CONTENTS

ANIMAL TRACKS
of the
Rocky Mountains

by Chris Stall

Idaho, Montana, Wyoming, Utah, Colorado,
Arizona and New Mexico

THE MOUNTAINEERS/SEATTLE

To Dianne.

The Mountaineers: Organized 1906 "... to explore, study, preserve, and enjoy the natural beauty of the Northwest."

6 5
5 4 3

Published by The Mountaineers
1011 S.W. Klickitat Way, Suite 107, Seattle, Washington 98134

Published simultaneously in Canada by Douglas & McIntyre, Ltd., 1615 Venables Street, Vancouver, B.C. V5L 2H1

Manufactured in the United States of America

Edited by Cathy Johnson
Book design by Betty Watson
Cover design by Nick Gregoric
Author photo by Angela Staubach
Track on cover: Mule deer

Library of Congress Cataloging-in-Publication Data
Stall, Chris.
  Animal tracks of the Rocky Mountains.

  Bibliography: p.
  Includes index.
  1. Animal tracks—Rocky Mountains. 2. Mammals—Rocky Mountains. 3. Birds—Rocky Mountains. I. Title.
QL719.R63S72   1989   599.0978   89-3332
ISBN 0-89886-185-3 (pbk.)

Preface

Most people don't get a chance to observe the animals in the wild, with the exceptions of road kills and a few nearly tame species in parks and campgrounds. Many wild animals are nocturnal or scarce, and many are shy and secretive to avoid the attention of predators, or stealthy as they stalk their next meal. In addition, most wild creatures are extremely wary of humans either instinctively or because they've learned through experience to be that way. We may catch fortuitous glimpses now and then, but few of us have the time or motivation required for lengthy journeys into wild country for the sole purpose of locating animals. The result is that areas where we would expect to see animals often seem practically devoid of wildlife.

That's rarely the case, of course. Actually, many animals reside in or pass through all reasonably wild habitats. Though we may not see them, they nevertheless leave indications of their passage. But for the most part such signs are obscure or confusing so that only the most experienced and knowledgeable wilderness travelers notice them.

There's one grand exception: *animal tracks.* Often readily apparent even to the most casual and inexperienced observer, tracks not only indicate the presence of wild animals but can also be matched relatively easily with the animals that made them. I guess that's why I have been fascinated by animal tracks since my childhood in rural New York, and why that focus has continued through two decades of wandering and searching for them in wild lands all across North America.

Animal Tracks of the Rocky Mountain States is a compilation of many years and many miles of my own field work, protracted observations, sketching, photography, and research into a list of articles and books too long to name and too heavy to carry into the back-country.

Animal tracks may be something you concern yourself with only when you happen on them, or your interest in tracks may become nearly obsessive. You may find yourself hiking with your chin resting securely on your chest, feverishly scanning the ground for clues. You may seek out snow because tracks show up on it better than most other surfaces. In the absence of snow, you might find yourself altering your routes, avoiding bedrock and ground cover, seeking out damp sand, soft dirt and mud along streams, near ponds and lakes, around swamps. You may journey into the desert in early morning, before the sand dries and moves on the wind. After a rainfall, you might make special trips to check fresh mud, even along dirt roads or hiking trails, knowing that among evidence of human activity the animal prints will be clear and precise.

Whatever your degree of interest, I hope you will enjoy using this book, in your backyard or in the wildest and most remote regions of the Rocky Mountain region, and that your interest in identifying tracks grows until you reach the level of knowledge at which you no longer need this book.

Good luck!

Chris Stall
Cincinnati, Ohio

Introduction

HOW TO USE THIS BOOK

1. When you first locate an unknown track, look around the immediate area to locate the clearest imprint (see Tracking Tips below). You can usually find at least one imprint or even a partial print distinct enough for counting toes, noting the shape of the heel pad, determining the presence or absence of claw marks, and so on.

2. Decide what kind of animal is most likely to have made the tracks; then turn to one of the two main sections of this book. The first and largest features mammals; the second, much shorter section is devoted entirely to birds.

3. Measure an individual track, using the ruler printed on the back cover of this book. Tracks of roughly five inches or less are illustrated life-size; those larger than five inches have been reduced as necessary to fit on the pages.

4. Flip quickly through the appropriate section until you find tracks that are about the same *size* as your mystery tracks. The tracks are arranged roughly by size from smallest to largest.

5. Search carefully for the tracks in the size range that, as closely as possible, match the *shape* of the unknown tracks.

6. If you find the right shape but the size depicted in the book is too big, remember that the illustrations represent tracks of an average *adult* animal. Perhaps your specimen was made by a young animal. Search some more: on the ground nearby you might locate the tracks of a parent, which will more closely match the size of the illustration.

7. Read the comments on range, habitat, and behavior, to help confirm the identification.

This book is intended to assist you in making field identifications of commonly encountered animal tracks. To keep the book compact, my remarks are limited to each animal's most obvious characteristics. By all means enhance your own knowledge of these track makers. Libraries and book stores are good places to begin learning more about wild animals. Visits to zoos with Rocky Mountain wildlife on display can also be worthwhile educational experiences. And there's no substitute for firsthand field study. You've found tracks, now you know what animals to look for. Read my notes on diet, put some bait out, sit quietly downwind with binoculars for a few hours, and see what comes along. Or follow the tracks a while. Use your imagination and common sense, and you'll be amazed at how much you can learn, and how rewarding the experiences can be.

As you use this book, remember that track identification is an inexact science. The illustrations in this book represent average *adult* tracks on *ideal* surfaces. But many of the tracks you encounter in the wild will be those of smaller-than-average animals, particularly in late spring and early summer. There are also larger-than-average animals, and injured or deformed ones, and animals that act unpredictably. Some creatures walk sideways on occasion. Most vary their gait so that in a single set of tracks front prints may fall ahead, behind, or beneath the rear. In addition, ground conditions are usually less than ideal in the wild, and animals often dislodge debris, which may further confuse the picture. Use this book as a guide, but anticipate lots of variations.

In attempting to identify tracks, remember that their size can vary greatly depending on the type of ground surface—sand that is loose or firm, wet or dry; a thin layer of mud over hard earth; deep soft mud; various lightly frozen surfaces; firm or loose dirt; dry or moist snow; a dusting of snow or frost over various surfaces; and so on. Note the surface from which the illustrations are taken and interpret what you find in nature accordingly.

You should also be aware that droplets from trees, windblown debris, and the like often leave a variety of marks on the ground that could be mistaken for animal tracks. While studying tracks, look around for and be aware of non-animal factors that might have left "tracks" of their own.

The range notes pertain only to the Rocky Mountain states of Idaho, Montana, Wyoming, Colorado, Utah, Arizona, and New Mexico. Many trackmakers in this book also live elsewhere in North America. Range and habitat remarks are general guidelines because both are subject to change, from variations in both animal and human populations, climatic factors, pollution levels, acts of God, and so forth.

The size, height, and weight listed for each animal are those for average adults. Size refers to length from nose to tip of tail; height, the distance from ground to shoulder.

A few well-known species have been left out of this book: moles and bats, for example, which leave no tracks. Animals that may be common elsewhere but are rare, or occur only in the margins of the Rocky Mountain region, have also been omitted. Some species herein, particularly small rodents and birds, stand as representatives of groups of related species. In such cases the featured species is the one most commonly encountered and widely distributed. Related species, often with similar tracks, are listed in the notes. Where their tracks can be distinguished, guidelines for doing so are provided.

If you encounter an injured animal or an apparently orphaned infant, you may be tempted to take it home and care for it. Do not do so. Instead, report the animal to local authorities, who are better able to care for it. In addition, federal and state laws often strictly control the handling of wild animals. This is always the case with species classified as *rare* or *endangered*. Animals are usually better left in the wild, and to do otherwise may be illegal.

TRACKING TIPS

At times you'll be lucky enough to find a perfectly clear and precise track that gives you all the information you need to identify the maker with a quick glance through this book. More often the track will be imperfect or fragmented. Following the tracks may lead you to a more readily identifiable print. Or maybe you have the time and inclination to follow an animal whose identity you already know in order to learn more about its habits, characteristics, and behavior.

Here are some tips for improving your tracking skills:

1. If you don't see tracks, look for disturbances—leaves or twigs in unnatural positions, debris or stones that appear to have been moved or turned. Stones become bleached on top over time, so a stone with its darker side up or sideways has recently been dislodged.

2. Push small sticks into the ground to mark individual signs. These will help you keep your bearings and "map out" the animal's general direction of travel.

3. Check immovable objects like trees, logs, and boulders along the route of travel for scratches, scuff marks, or fragments of hair.

4. Look at the ground from different angles, from standing height, from kneeling height and, if possible, from an elevated position in a tree or on a boulder or rise.

5. On very firm surfaces, place your cheek on the ground and observe the surface, first through one eye, then the other, looking for unnatural depressions or disturbances.

6. Study the trail from as many different directions as possible. Trail signs may become obvious as the angle of light between them and your eyes changes, especially if dew, dust, or rain covers some parts of the ground surface.

7. Check for tracks beneath recently disturbed leaves or fallen debris.

8. Try not to focus your attention so narrowly that you lose sight of the larger patterns of the country around you.

9. Keep your bearings. Some animals circle back if they become aware of being followed. If you find yourself following signs in a circular path, try waiting motionless and silent for a while, observing behind you.

10. Look ahead as far as possible as you follow signs. Animals take the paths of least resistance, so look for trails or runways. You may even catch sight of your quarry.

11. Animals are habitual in their movements between burrows, den sites, sources of water and food, temporary shelters, prominent trees, and so on. As you track and look ahead, try to anticipate where the creature might be going.

12. Stalk as you track; move as carefully and quietly as possible.

The secrets to successful tracking are patience and knowledge. Whenever you see an animal leaving tracks, go look at them and note the activity you observed. When you find and identify tracks, make little sketches alongside the book's illustrations, showing cluster patterns, or individual impressions that are different from those drawn. Make notes about what you learn in the wilds and from other readings. Eventually, you will build a body of knowledge from your own experience, and your future attempts at track identification will become easier and more certain.

This book is largely a compilation of the author's personal experiences. Your experiences with certain animals and their tracks may be identical, similar, or quite different. If you notice a discrepancy or find tracks that are not included in this book, carefully note your observations, or even amend the illustrations or text to reflect your own experiences. This book is intended for use in the field as a tool for identiying animal tracks of the Rocky Mountain region.

Mammals

DEER MOUSE   *Peromyscus maniculatus*

Order: Rodentia (gnawing mammals). **Family:** Cricetidae (New World rats and mice). **Range and habitat:** common throughout all Rocky Mountain states; in woods, prairies, rocks; and nearly all other dry-land areas. **Size and weight:** 8 inches; 1 ounce. **Diet:** omnivorous, primarily seeds but also mushrooms and other fungi, berries, herbs, insects, larvae, and carrion. **Sounds:** occasional faint chirps, squeaks and chattering.

The abundant, wide-ranging, and familiar deer mouse is a medium-sized long-tailed mouse with pretty white underside, feet, pointy nose, and fairly large ears. Though primarily a mouse of the wilds, it is occasionally found in both abandoned and occupied buildings as well. A good climber, the deer mouse is active year round, generally nocturnal, and adaptable to many habitats. It makes up the main diet of many carnivorous birds and mammals, but is not so completely defenseless, as you might think. . . it may bite if handled carelessly.

The deer mouse usually leaves a distinctive track pattern—four-print clusters about 1.5 inches wide, walking or leaping up to 9 inches, with the tail dragging. As with any creature so small, its tracks are distinct only on rare occasions when surface conditions are perfect. More often you find merely clusters of tiny dimples in the mud or snow.

Such tracks could also be made by other "white-footed mice" (e.g., cactus, canyon, brush, pinon, or rock mice) or even by other, more distantly related mice (e.g., house, harvest, or grasshopper mice). Give or take an inch and a few fractions of an ounce, they're all quite similar in appearance. You will need a good pictorial field guide and some patient field work to make positive identifications. Mouse tracks, however, can be distinguished from those of the shrews, whose feet are about the same size: mouse track clusters are wider than those of shrews, and shrews tend to scuttle along or burrow under snow, rather than run and leap. If you follow mouse tracks, more often than not they will lead to evidence of seed eating; shrews are strictly carnivorous.

12

Deer Mouse
life size in mud

13

SOUTHERN RED-BACKED VOLE   *Clethrionomys gapperi*
Boreal vole, Gapper redback vole, red-backed mouse

Order: Rodentia (gnawing mammals). **Family:** Cricetidae (New World mice and rats). **Range and habitat:** all Rocky Mountain states, but more common farther north; in cool, damp forests and swampy fringe areas. **Size and weight:** 6 inches; 1 ounce. **Diet:** primarily vegetarian, including berries, herbs, nuts, seeds, lichens, and fungi; occasionally insects. **Sounds:** rarely audible to humans.

Voles, out and about by day, can frequently be glimpsed scurrying around. Though mouselike in habits, voles are squatter and plumper than mice, with no obvious neck and a slightly shorter and bushier tail. They are active year round, day and night, and are good climbers. Of all the voles present within the Rocky Mountain states, the southern red-backed vole is the only one with an easily distinguishable characteristic, its reddish back.

Several voles of the genus *Microtus*, including the mountain, meadow, long-tailed, Richardson's, sagebrush, and Mexican voles, occupy ranges that overlap that of the red-backed vole and so closely resemble it (and one another) that positive identification of the animals, or their tracks, is difficult in the field.

Vole tracks are generally distinctive as a group because vole feet are peculiarly shaped and voles tend to walk and sit rather than run and leap like mice. Southern red-backed voles usually travel on the surface, while meadow voles generally live in denser vegetation and burrow along intricate systems of runways, which they often carefully line with cuttings of grass. Then again, Southern red-backed voles occasionally do that also. The mountain vole is often found at higher elevations, and the long-tailed vole... yes, it usually has a slightly longer tail, which may leave telltale marks. Honestly, though, if you haven't caught sight of that rust-colored fur, you might just want to settle for knowing the tracks were made by a generic vole and save your speculations for more potentially discernible subjects.

14

Southern Red-backed Vole
life size in mud

DUSKY SHREW   *Sorex obscurus*

Order: Insectivora (insect-eating mammals, including shrews, moles, and bats). **Family:** Soricidae (shrews). **Range and habitat:** portions of all Rocky Mountain states except Arizona; very adaptable; in marshes and fringe areas near water, and in coniferous forests, dry hillsides, and heather. **Size and weight:** 5 inches; 1 ounce. **Diet:** slugs, snails, spiders, insects, and larvae; occasionally mice and carrion. **Sounds:** commonly silent.

Shrews are vole-shaped creatures, but with shorter legs, a slightly more elongated body, and a long pointed snout. Shrew dentists have a big advantage in distinguishing the various species, because variations in unicuspid teeth are all that differentiate many of them. *All* shrews are little eating machines, though, with extremely high metabolism, evidenced by heartbeat and respiration rates around 1200 per minute. In fact, shrews consume more than their own body weight in food on a daily basis.

The shrews' constant and aggressive quest for food makes their tracks, in general, fairly easy to identify. The animals move around with more single-minded purpose than mice or voles, usually in a series of short hops in which the rear feet fall over the tracks of the front feet; the tails often drag, leaving the distinctive pattern shown, usually less than an inch in width. When individual impressions are more distinct, you may notice that shrews have five toes on both fore- and hind feet (most micelike creatures have four toes on the forefeet).

The dusky shrew is the most adaptable of the Rocky Mountain shrews; active both day and night and slightly larger than other shrews, it tends to leave the best track imprints in the most places. Dusky shrews often occupy dry habitats; if you find similar tracks in moist habitats, they may belong to either the dusky or the vagrant shrew, nearly identical animals. In arid, low deserts or sagebrush, shrew tracks could be those of Merriam's shrew or the desert shrew. The northern water shrew lives along small, cold mountain streams, and the masked shrew tends to be secretive and nocturnal. Then again, the uncommon, but wide-ranging, dwarf shrew might just have made the tracks. At least the generic shrew *pattern* is unique!

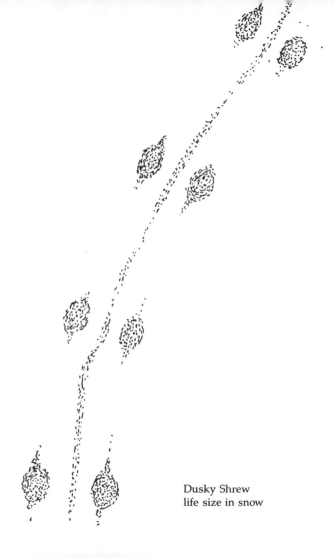

Dusky Shrew
life size in snow

WESTERN JUMPING MOUSE   *Zapus princeps*

Order: Rodentia (gnawing mammals). **Family:** Zapodidae (jumping mice). **Range and habitat:** portions of all Rocky Mountain states west of the Continental Divide; in lush grassy areas at medium to higher elevations in mountains, near water systems, and mountain meadow fringes. **Size and weight:** 9 inches; 1 ounce. **Diet:** vegetarian, including grasses, seeds, berries, and fungi. **Sounds:** frequent chirps at night between members of foraging groups.

The western jumping mouse varies in color from yellowish to reddish, with a very long tail and relatively large, strong hind legs and feet. It is not easy to sight in the wild because it is generally nocturnal during warm weather and hibernates for 6 to 8 months during the long, cold winters of its high-elevation habitats.

The tracks of this jumping mouse are quite distinctive and should be easy to identify, even if the imprints are not very clear, because it is the only mouse living in the habitat described above that takes single jumps, or several in a series, of 3 to 5 feet each. Rear-foot impressions will be noticeably longer (around half an inch) than those of other similar-sized creatures, and its long tail leaves marks more frequently (either among the footprints or out to the side). But when leaping in a series of bounds, only the hind feet contact the ground, leaving a trail of small, widely spaced print-pairs without tail drag marks, also unique.

The meadow jumping mouse is very similar, but it generally inhabits flatlands, and is found only east of the Great Divide. The only other small jumpers in the Rocky Mountain states are pocket and kangaroo mice and kangaroo rats, all of which live primarily in dry sagebrush regions, where tracking is difficult.

Western Jumping Mouse
life size in mud

LEAST CHIPMUNK   *Eutamias minimus*

Order: Rodentia (gnawing mammals). **Family:** Sciuridae (squirrels). **Range and habitat:** portions of all Rocky Mountain states; from low sagebrush deserts and rocky areas with scattered trees to coniferous and mixed forests and adjacent chaparral at all altitudes, common in parks and camping areas. **Size and weight:** 8 inches; 2 ounces. **Diet:** vegetation, berries, grains, seeds, insects, and carrion. **Sounds:** shrill and persistent "chip, chip."

The most widespread chipmunk species in the Rocky Mountain states, the least chipmunk is difficult to distinguish from several other locally common chipmunks, including the yellow-pine, cliff, Colorado, red-tailed, and Uinta. All have more or less distinctive black and white stripes from nose to their moderately bushy tail, and they chatter nearly constantly as they leap and scurry over the ground and up and down tree trunks during the daylight hours.

The track patterns of chipmunks are roughly 2 inches in width, with 7 to 15 inches between clusters of prints. Chipmunks often run up on their toes, so rear-heel imprints may not show at all or may be less clear. The hind-foot tracks (five-toed) almost always fall in front of the forefoot tracks (four-toed), typical of all squirrel-family members. If you find tracks like these in midwinter, however, you can assume they were left by a small squirrel rather than a chipmunk, because chipmunks tend to hole up with food caches in winter. If they are indeed chipmunk tracks, you will probably catch sight of the maker, because chipmunks are noisy and not all that timid, particularly in campgrounds; in fact, they will more than likely approach you for a handout.

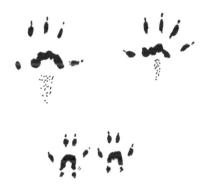

Least Chipmunk
life size in mud

RED SQUIRREL   *Tamiasciurus hudsonicus*

Order: Rodentia (gnawing mammals). **Family:** Sciuridae (squirrels). **Range and habitat:** portions of all Rocky Mountain states; in coniferous or mixed forests and occasionally nearby in swamp fringes. **Size and weight:** 12 inches; 8 ounces. **Diet:** nuts, fungi, insects, larvae, cones, seeds, and vegetation. **Sounds:** a great variety of noisy, ratchetlike sounds.

The red squirrel is the only Rocky Mountain tree squirrel that is active during the day year round. Quite common throughout most of its range, this small, noisy squirrel is easy to identify by its rust or grayish-red coat of fur, fluffy rust-colored tail, and the white rings around its eyes. It lives in ground burrows as well as in downed logs and standing trees and is particularly fond of pine cones, which it shucks for the seeds, leaving piles of cone remnants everywhere. Occasionally in the fall, you may be startled by green cones falling systematically and seemingly unaided from tall coniferous trees. The red squirrel is up there, out of sight, cutting the cones; later it will gather them from the forest floor and hide them away for the cold months to come.

The red squirrel has long, curved toenails that act as hooks for tree climbing and which often leave definite imprints. Clear tracks show the squirrel's four toes on its front feet, and the five toes on its hind feet, which usually fall ahead of the front. Often the heel marks will be absent because the red squirrel is usually running quickly and nervously when it is on the ground; the track spacing may vary widely, with leaps from 8 to 30 inches. Individual prints may be as long as 1.5 inches.

Red Squirrel
life size in mud

GOLDEN-MANTLED
GROUND SQUIRREL
Spermophilus lateralis
Picket pin, copperhead, flickertail

Order: Rodentia (gnawing mammals). **Family:** Sciuridae (squirrels). **Range and habitat:** mountainous areas of all Rocky Mountain states; in chaparral and in semiopen coniferous forests to and above timberline. **Size and weight:** 12 inches; 9 ounces. **Diet:** omnivorous, including herbs, seeds, fruits, insects, eggs, and carrion. **Sounds:** usually silent; shrill and rapid chirps signal alarm.

The ground squirrels of the Rocky Mountain states vary greatly in appearance and habits, but they all are *terrestrial*, living in extensive burrow systems. They tend to stand up and whistle or trill when alarmed, rather than chattering like their arboreal cousins. Some are solitary, others colonial. Most hibernate 7 or 8 months of the year, but even when active rarely venture far from their burrows.

The most wide-ranging of the Rocky Mountain species, the attractive golden-mantled ground squirrel has the lateral black and white body stripes of a chipmunk, but is a good deal larger and has no facial stripes.

The track shape and pattern of the golden-mantled ground squirrel is common to most ground squirrels. The truncated inner toe of the front foot may leave only a slight or no imprint. Nine to 18 inches separate groups of four prints made by running animals; they usually walk only at den entrances. Ground squirrels tend to be more flatfooted than tree squirrels, and whereas tree squirrel tracks are never far from trees and usually lead to or away from them, ground squirrel tracks always lead to or from the squirrels' subterranean homes. The toes, adapted for digging, tend to leave splayed prints; and the claws often leave imprints farther from the toes. A final clue: ground squirrels almost never leave tracks in snow; they are too busy sleeping away the winter.

Other Rocky Mountain ground squirrels with similar tracks include white-tailed and black-tailed prairie dogs, rock squirrel, and Belding's, Columbian, Richardson's, Townsend's, Uinta, thirteen-lined and Washington ground squirrels.

Golden-mantled Ground Squirrel
life size in mud

PIKA   *Ochotona princeps*
Cony

Order: Lagomorpha (rabbitlike mammals). **Family:** Ochotonidae (pikas). **Range and habitat:** mountainous portions of all Rocky Mountain states except Arizona; in scree slopes and rock slides, usually from 6000 feet above sea level up to timberline. **Size and weight:** 8 inches; 6 ounces. **Diet:** grasses, and herbaceous vegetation. **Sounds:** series of short squeaks, warning of danger.

In scree slopes along the highway in Glacier National Park, travelers often see chipmunks, ground squirrels, and pikas together, but there's no mistaking pikas, little grayish-brown furballs with short round ears and no tail showing, usually sitting quietly in the sun on a promontory or moving quite fluidly over the rocky shards. Pikas spend their summers making little haystacks of clipped vegetation that dry in the sun among the rocks. The hay serves as food supplies for the winter, when the pika remains active but often stays below the snow surface. Its peculiar call is also distinctive and might puzzle you when you hear it coming up from beneath a deep snow cover.

Pika tracks are not easy to locate because this small relative of rabbits and hares lives primarily among rocks and—in winter—beneath snow surfaces, but occasionally you will find them on early-fall or late-spring snow, or in mud around alpine ponds near the animal's stony home. The pika's hairy feet and toes—five front and four rear—and shuffling gait produce what looks like miniature bear tracks; its running trails are composed of clusters not more than 3 inches wide and usually about 10 inches apart.

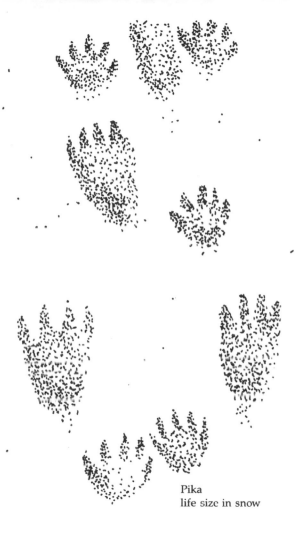

Pika
life size in snow

SHORT-TAILED WEASEL
LONG-TAILED WEASEL

Mustela erminea
Mustela frenata

Order: Carnivora (flesh-eating mammals). **Family:** Mustelidae (the weasel family). **Range and habitat:** widespread throughout five northern Rocky Mountain states, rare or absent in New Mexico and Arizona; in varied grasslands, wetlands, farmlands, and brushy or wooded terrain to above timberline; usually near water. **Size and weight:** 12 inches; 6 ounces. **Diet:** rodents, including chipmunks, ground squirrels, and mice; occasionally moles. **Sounds:** generally silent; occasionally squeals.

The short-tailed weasel is an inquisitive and aggressive little carnivore with a thin, elongated body and short, bushy tail. Brown with a white underside and feet during the summer months, in winter the weasel turns almost entirely white, save for the tip of its tail, which remains black. In this fur the short-tailed weasel is commonly known as an ermine.

Short-tailed weasels, like all mustelids, have five toes on each foot, but the imprint of the fifth may be absent. They bound around on the ground most of the time, but also walk along fallen logs, climb trees, and chase prey into water. Usually the rear feet fall over the imprints of the front feet, leaving a line of double tracks distinctive of the smaller weasels. Sometimes, weasels may also leave a variety of track clusters as they dart about searching for food.

The long-tailed weasel, a slightly larger version of the ermine, occupies the same range. The tracks of the two species can be differentiated as follows: ermine track clusters are about 2 inches wide and not much more than 13 inches apart when running; long-tailed weasel track clusters are as much as 3 inches wide by 4 inches long, with up to 20 inches between clusters.

Long-tailed Weasel
life size in mud

NORTHERN FLYING SQUIRREL   *Glaucomys sabrinus*

Order: Rodentia (gnawing mammals). **Family:** Sciuridae (squirrels). **Range and habitat:** portions of Montana, Idaho, and Utah, rare in western Colorado; in coniferous and, occasionally, mixed forests at higher altitudes. **Size and weight:** 11 inches; 6 ounces. **Diet:** bark, fungi, lichen, seeds, insects, eggs, and carrion. **Sounds:** generally silent; occasionally makes chirpy, birdlike noises.

The northern flying squirrel is one of only two species of tree squirrels found in the Rocky Mountain states, the other being the red squirrel (see following discussion). Northern flying squirrels are nocturnal, so chances are you will only see their tracks, unless you happen to knock against or cut down one of the hollow trees in which they are fond of nesting; in that case, if the squirrel that runs out is gray, you've had a rare glimpse of the northern flying squirrel.

During summer, the northern flying squirrel doesn't leave much evidence of its passage. It lives mostly in trees, using the fur-covered membrane that extends along each side of its body from the front to the rear legs to glide between trees and occasionally from tree to earth, where it usually leaves no marks on the ground cover of its forest habitat. On snow-covered surfaces, however, its tracks can be identified because they lead away from what looks like a miniature, scuffed snow-angel, the pattern left when the squirrel lands at the end of an aerial descent. The tracks may wander around a bit if the squirrel has foraged for morsels, but they will lead back to the trunk of a nearby tree before long.

Northern Flying Squirrel
life size in snow

BUSHY-TAILED WOODRAT   *Neotoma cinerea*
Cave rat, pack rat

Order: Rodentia (gnawing mammals). **Family:** Cricetidae (New World rats and mice). **Range and habitat:** widespread throughout Rocky Mountain states; in coniferous forests, cliffs, caves, rocky areas at all elevations, and occasionally in abandoned buildings; avoids deserts. **Size and weight:** 15 inches; 20 ounces. **Diet:** vegetarian, supplemented with insects, eggs, carrion when available. **Sounds:** occasionally drums and thumps feet.

This native American rat is active year round but it is seldom sighted in the wild, as it is generally nocturnal and frequents rugged terrain. The bushy-tailed woodrat is slightly larger than the imported Norway and black rats and has a fluffy, not scaly, tail. Unlike Norway and black rats, woodrats avoid humans and their habitations, although they may "borrow" shiny and other attractive objects from abandoned buildings or active campsites within their territories.

Like other woodrats, the pretty bushy-tailed woodrat is a skilled and frequent climber and often builds large nests of sticks, bones, and other refuse in trees or cliffs, or on the ground in clumps of brush. It could be mistaken for a gray squirrel with prominent ears, but no gray squirrels reside within the Rocky Mountain states.

Other woodrats present in Rocky Mountain states are the white-throated, desert, Mexican and Southern Plains woodrats. All are typically ratlike—without the bushy squirrel-like tail—and are found only in dry brushland or desert areas in southern areas of the region.

The bushy-tailed woodrat has fairly stubby toes, four on the fore feet and five on the hind, that usually leave uniquely shaped tracks with no claw marks. The tracks are roughly in line when walking and grouped as illustrated when running, with 8 or more inches separating the clusters of prints. Like most small rodents, when woodrats leap, their front feet land first, followed by the back feet which come down ahead of the front imprints, providing the spring into the next leap. If the characteristic stubby-toed imprints are not clear, the short spacing relative to foot size should help distinguish woodrat tracks from similar ones made by other animals of comparable size.

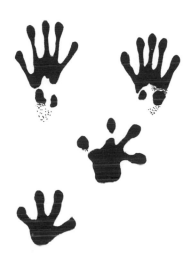

Bushy-tailed Woodrat
life size in mud

MINK

Mustela vison

Order: Carnivora (flesh-eating mammals). **Family:** Mustelidae (the weasel family). **Range:** throughout Idaho, Montana, Wyoming, Colorado, and parts of Utah; in brushy or open forested areas along streams, lakes, and other wetlands. **Size and weight:** 24 inches; 3 pounds. **Diet:** primarily muskrats and smaller mammals; also birds, frogs, fish, crayfish, and eggs. **Sounds:** snarls, squeals, and hisses.

The mink is about the size of a small cat and medium brown all over. It is an excellent swimmer and may wander several miles a day searching for food along stream- and riverbanks and around the shorelines of lakes. Its den, too, is usually in a stream- or riverbank, an abandoned muskrat nest, or otherwise near water. Generally a nocturnal hunter, its tracks are likely to be the only indication you will have of its presence.

Intermediate in size between a long-tailed weasel and marten, the mink leaves either groups of four tracks like those illustrated or the characteristic double pair of tracks, usually not more than 26 inches apart. The tracks nearly always run along the edge of water. Though it has five toes both front and rear, it is quite common for only four toed imprints to be apparent. Like all mustelids, the mink employs its scent glands to mark territory; so, as you track it through its hunting ranges, you may notice a strong scent here and there, different but as potent as that of its relative the skunk. You might also, in snow, find signs of prey being dragged, invariably leading to the animal's den.

Mink
life size in mud

WESTERN SPOTTED SKUNK
Civet cat, hydrophobia cat

Spilogale gracilis

Order: Carnivora (flesh-eating mammals). **Family:** Mustelidae (the weasel family). **Range and habitat:** widespread in all Rocky Mountain states, except rare in or absent from central Montana; in brushy or sparsely wooded areas along streams, among boulders, and in prairies. **Size and weight:** 25 inches; 3 pounds. **Diet:** omnivorous, including rats, mice, birds, insects, eggs, carrion, seeds, fruit, and occasionally vegetation. **Sounds:** usually silent.

The spotted skunks are the smallest and most visually interesting of the North American skunks. About the size of a small housecat, with an assortment of white spots and streaks over its black coat, the spotted skunk has finer, silkier fur than the other skunks, is quicker and more agile, and occasionally climbs trees, although it doesn't stay aloft for long. Like all skunks, it is primarily nocturnal, but you might see it at dawn or dusk, or foraging during the daylight in winter, when hunger keeps it active. Skunks have the most highly effective scent glands of all the mustelids and can, when severely provoked, shoot a fine spray of extremely irritating methyl mercaptan as far as 25 feet.

Skunk tracks are all similar, with five toes on each foot leaving prints, toenail prints commonly visible, and front tracks slightly less flat-footed than rear. Only size and irregular stride may help distinguish the tracks of the spotted skunk from those of the twice-as-large striped skunk, which is widespread and common throughout the Rocky Mountain states. Spotted skunk tracks will be about 1.25 inches long at most; adult striped skunks leave tracks up to 2 inches in length. On the other hand, the quick spotted skunk leaves a foot or more between *clusters* of prints when running, while the larger striped skunk lopes along with only about 5 or 6 inches between more strung-out track groups.

Because skunks can hold most land animals at bay with their formidible scent, owls are their chief predators. If you are following a skunk trail that ends suddenly, perhaps a bit of black and white fur remaining mysteriously where the tracks disappear, you might be able to guess what transpired.

Western Spotted Skunk
life size in mud

MUSKRAT   *Ondatra zibethicus*

Order: Rodentia (gnawing mammals). **Family:** Cricetidae (New World rats and mice). **Range and habitat:** widespread throughout all Rocky Mountain states, except in the arid southern regions; in streams, lakes, ponds, and marshes. **Size and weight:** 24 inches; 4 pounds. **Diet:** aquatic vegetation; occasionally shellfish and small aquatic animals. **Sounds:** high-pitched squeaks.

The muskrat is a large brown rat with a volelike appearance, modified for its aquatic life by a rudderlike scaly tail and partially webbed hind feet. Muskrats associate readily with beavers and occasionally nest within the superstructure of beaver lodges. More often, muskrats burrow into riverbanks or construct lodges similar to those of beavers but extending only a couple of feet above water level and composed of aquatic vegetation, primarily grasses and reeds, rather than trees. Muskrat lodges always have underwater entrances. Mainly nocturnal, the muskrat can be seen during the late afternoon or at dusk, pulling the V of its ripples across a still water surface, tail skulling behind, mouth full of grass for supper or nest-building.

Muskrat tracks are nearly always found in mud close to water. The muskrat is one of the few rodents with five toes on its front feet, but its truncated inner toes often leave no imprint. It leaves tracks about 2 inches apart when walking to 12 inches apart when running, with the tail sometimes dragging as well. The track of the hind foot is usually more distinctive than that of the front, and the stiff webbing of hair between the toes is often visible.

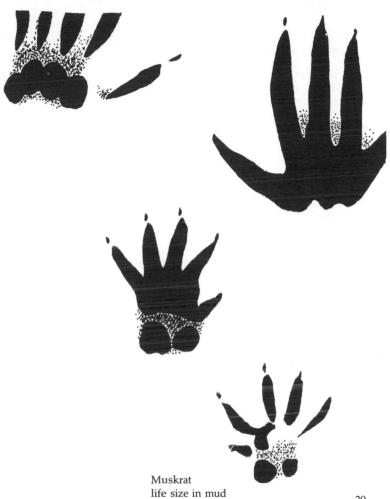

Muskrat
life size in mud

YELLOW-BELLIED MARMOT   *Marmota flaviventris*
Mountain marmot, rockchuck, whistler

Order: Rodentia (gnawing mammals). **Family:** Sciuridae (squirrels). **Range and habitat:** mountainous portions of all Rocky Mountain states, rare in northern Arizona and New Mexico; among talus and rocky outcroppings in valleys, foothills, and mountainous regions, up to about 12,000 feet elevation. **Size and weight:** 18 inches; 10 pounds. **Diet:** prefers alfalfa; also succulent alpine grasses, plants, and flowers. **Sounds:** loud and high-pitched chirps at short intervals, and whistles.

The yellow-bellied marmot is a large, pretty American ground squirrel covered with light blond fur, with a distinctly yellowish neck and belly. Marmots lead lives of inertia, hibernating from August or September through February or March, sleeping at night during the short high-country summer, and spending the daytime eating or sunbathing on prominent lookout rocks. Fairly easy to find in the mountains, marmots betray their presence with piercing whistles, employed as both an alarm and to keep tabs on fellow marmots' locations. Their eyesight is not particularly good; by staying downwind and moving slowly, you should have no trouble sneaking up on them for a closer look.

When they walk, yellow-bellied marmots leave tracks that often intermingle and overlap. The illustration shows the four toes of the front foot and the five of the rear, a configuration typical of rodents. The rear foot is actually larger than the front one, but very often, especially when the marmot is running, the heel does not touch the ground. For this reason, the hind-foot track could be mistaken for the front footprint of a small raccoon, except that raccoons have five toes on each foot. Typically, yellow-bellied marmot tracks are less than 2 inches long, with from 3 to 14 inches between clusters, depending on the speed of movement. Don't look for them on snow; marmots will be asleep through the snow season.

The hoary marmot lives in mountainous northern Idaho and western Montana. Tracks of the hoary marmot are identical to those of the yellow-bellied in shape, but are usually well over 2.5 inches long, with greater distance between running tracks.

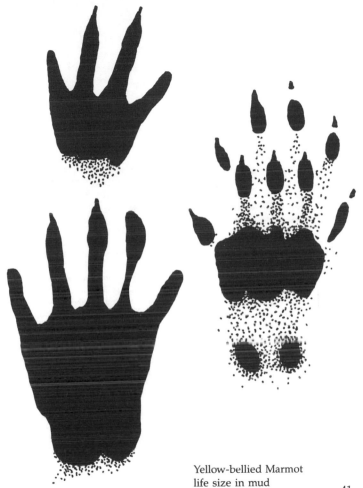

Yellow-bellied Marmot
life size in mud

41

MARTEN
Martes americana
Pine marten, American sable

Order: Carnivora (flesh-eating mammals). **Family:** Mustelidae (the weasel family). **Range and habitat:** mountainous portions of all Rocky Mountain states except Arizona; in coniferous forests, occasionally in adjoining areas, including rock slides. **Size and weight:** 30 inches; 3 pounds. **Diet:** primarily red squirrels; also other small mammals, birds, eggs, berries, and nuts. **Sounds:** generally silent.

Between a mink and a fisher in size, the energetic and adaptable marten is typically weasel-shaped, buff-colored on its throat and brownish or rusty-brown over the rest of its body, with a long, fluffy tail. Solitary, generally nocturnal, and always extremely wary, it is seldom sighted in the wild, but it is also inquisitive and can be lured from its den with squeaking, mouselike noises made by kissing the back of your hand. The marten covers distances of many miles in a single night's hunting and is active year round. A skillful tree climber, it spends a lot of time off the ground and often dens in tree cavities; the marten can nearly always be found in forests the red squirrel inhabits.

The marten leaves few signs in the summer forest except for scat stations, spots where droppings are repeatedly left. On snow, its tracks are very similar to but slightly larger than mink tracks. Small, thin pads behind five toes and nails are normally visible in marten tracks, with size and spacing somewhat larger than that of the mink. Marten tracks, however, will tend to lead to and from trees and rarely venture near water, unlike the mink's. Walking tracks are usually 6 to 9 inches apart, running clusters 24 inches apart, and bounding pairs of overlapping prints as much as 40 inches apart.

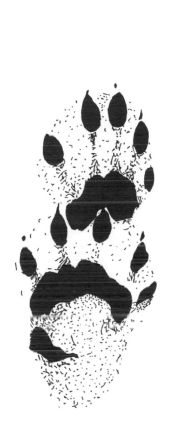

Marten
life size in mud

BOBCAT
Wildcat

Felis rufus

Order: Carnivora (flesh-eating mammals). **Family:** Felidae (cats). **Range and habitat:** throughout all Rocky Mountain states; in forested foothills, swamps and fringes, rimrock, and chaparral. **Size and weight:** 30 inches; 35 pounds. **Diet:** small mammals and birds; rarely carrion. **Sounds:** less vocal than the lynx, but capable of generic cat family range of noises.

Closely related to the lynx, the bobcat is a very adaptable feline, afield both day and night and wandering as much as 50 miles in a day of hunting, occasionally into suburban areas. It is primarily a ground hunter, but will climb trees and drop onto unexpecting prey if the opportunity presents itself. You could mistake it for a large tabby cat with a bobbed tail, but the similarity ends there, for the bobcat has quite a wild disposition combined with much greater size, strength and razor-sharp claws and teeth.

You can expect to encounter bobcat tracks almost anywhere. You'll know the roundish tracks belong to a cat because the rectractile claws never leave imprints and the toes usually spread a bit more than a dog's. Bobcat tracks are too large to be mistaken for those of a domestic cat, however. The animal's weight will have set the tracks deeper in a soft surface than you would expect from a housecat, and domestic cats have pads that are single-lobed at the front end. Bobcat tracks are clearly smaller than those of a lynx or mountain lion and are therefore easily identifiable by process of elimination.

Bobcat
life size in mud

GRAY FOX

Urocyon cinereoargenteus

Order: Carnivora (flesh-eating mammals). **Family:** Canidae (dogs). **Range and habitat:** portions of Utah, Colorado, Arizona, and New Mexico, in chaparral and brushy, sparsely wooded rimrock country. **Size and weight:** 40–42 inches; 12–15 pounds. **Diet:** omnivorous, including small mammals, birds, insects, eggs, fruit, nuts, grains, and other forage. **Sounds:** normally silent; occasionally short barking yips.

This pretty fox with gray back, rusty flanks, and white underside is generally more nocturnal and secretive than the red fox, but you might spot one foraging by daylight in thick foliage or forested areas. The only canine in America with the ability to climb, it frequently seeks refuge and food in trees, but cottontails are the mainstay of its diet when they are available. The gray fox typically dens among boulders on the slopes of rocky ridges or in rock piles, hollow logs, or the like; unlike the red fox, it uses these dens in winter as well as summer.

Gray fox tracks are very similar to those of the red fox, except that the prints are usually more distinct due to the relative lack of fur on the animal's feet. The tracks always show the imprints of claws and may be the same size or slightly smaller and narrower than the red fox's, with 7 to 12 inches between walking prints.

Gray Fox
life size in mud

RED FOX

Vulpes vulpes

Order: Carnivora (flesh-eating mammals). **Family:** Canidae (dogs). **Range and habitat:** all Rocky Mountain states, in woodlands, open fringes, and especially in mountainous areas near timberland. **Size and weight:** 40–42 inches; 12–15 pounds. **Diet:** omnivorous, including small mammals, birds, insects, eggs, fruit, nuts, grains, and other forage. **Sounds:** a variety of doglike noises.

The sleek little red fox usually leaves a distinctive, nearly straight line of tracks, the front track slightly wider than the rear. Its feet are quite furry, adapted to the generally higher elevations of its habitat; as a result the prints of pads and toes are often indistinct unless the surface is quite firm, in which case only a partial pad imprint will appear, making the toe prints clearly separate. The claws always leave marks, although in deep snow the tail may brush over and obscure some of the finer points of the tracks. Red fox tracks could be mistaken for those of a small domestic dog, except that the fox's heel pad has a unique curved bar and the heel pads of domestic dogs tend to be longer, extending forward between the outer toes. Also, a walking red fox leaves tracks from 12 to 18 inches apart, a somewhat longer stride than that of a similar-sized domestic dog.

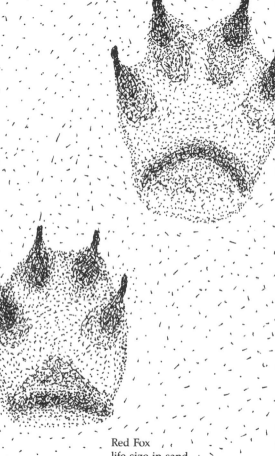

Red Fox
life size in sand

COYOTE
Brush wolf, prairie wolf

Canis latrans

Order: Carnivora (flesh-eating mammals). **Family:** Canidae (dogs). **Range and habitat:** widespread throughout all Rocky Mountain states; primarily in prairies, open woodlands, and brushy fringes, but very adaptable; can turn up anywhere. **Size and weight:** 48 inches; 45 pounds. **Diet:** omnivorous, including rodents and other small mammals, fish, carrion, insects, berries, grains, nuts, and vegetation. **Sounds:** wide range of canine sounds; most often heard yelping in group chorus late at night.

An important controller of small rodents, the smart, adaptable coyote is—unlike the gray wolf—steadily expanding its range. About the size of a collie, the coyote is a good runner and swimmer and has great stamina. Despite its wide range, it is shy, and you will be lucky to see one in the wild.

Typically canine, the coyote's front paw is slightly larger than the rear, and the front toes tend to spread wider, though not as wide as the bobcat's. The toenails nearly always leave imprints. The shape of coyote pads is unique, the front pads differing markedly from the rear, as shown, and the outer toes are usually slightly larger than the inner toes on each foot. The coyote tends to walk in a straight line and keep its tail down, which often leaves an imprint in deep snow. These characteristics plus walking strides of 8 to 16 inches and leaps to 10 feet may help you distinguish coyote tracks from those of domestic dogs with feet of the same size.

Coyote
life size in mud

BADGER

Taxidea taxus

Order: Carnivora (flesh-eating mammals). **Family:** Mustelidae (the weasel family). **Range and habitat:** widespread throughout all Rocky Mountain states; in treeless meadows, semiopen prairies, grasslands, and deserts at all altitudes, wherever ground-dwelling rodents are abundant. **Size and weight:** 28 inches; 20 pounds. **Diet:** carnivorous, including all smaller rodents, snakes, birds, eggs, insects, and carrion. **Sounds:** may snarl or hiss when alarmed or annoyed.

The badger is a solitary creature that digs up most of its food and tunnels into the earth to escape danger. Its powerful short legs and long strong claws are well suited to its earth-moving ways, and badgers can reputedly dig faster than a man with a shovel. Above ground the badger is a fierce fighter threatened only by much larger carnivores. The animal is active in daylight and not too shy, even entering campgrounds in its search for food. Its facial markings are quite distinctive and easily recognized: the face is black with white ears and cheeks and a white stripe running from its nose over the top of its head. The rest of the body is light brown or gray, and the feet are black.

Badger tracks show five long, clear toe prints of each foot and obvious marks left by the long front claws. The animal walks on its soles, which may or may not leave complete prints. Its pigeon-toed trail may be confused with the porcupine's in deep snow, but a porcupine trail will invariably lead to a tree or into a natural den, a badger's to a burrow of its own excavation; another clue: the badger's short, soft tail rarely leaves a mark.

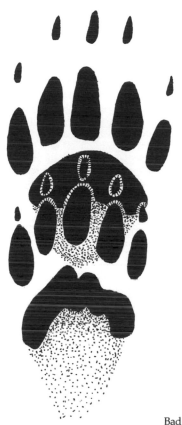

Badger
life size in mud

FISHER
Black cat

Martes pennanti

Order: Carnivora (flesh-eating mammals). **Family:** Mustelidae (the weasel family). **Range and habitat:** portions of western Montana and Wyoming, northern Idaho; in coniferous and mixed forests and occasionally in cutover areas, usually at lower elevations. **Size and weight:** 36 inches; 15 pounds. **Diet:** primarily smaller mammals, including porcupines; also insects, birds, eggs, fish, frogs, and, infrequently, fruit and vegetation. **Sounds:** hisses, growls, and snarls.

The fisher likes fish when it finds them washed ashore, but will not enter water to catch them. This dark brown weasel with its foot-long bushy, tapering tail is slightly larger than the marten, more adaptable in habitat, and wider ranging, covering a territory of 150 square miles or more. Very aggressive and strong for its size, the fisher is terrifically speedy whether on the ground or climbing, all of which may explain why it is among the few predators that kill and eat porcupines regularly. Its diet also includes other weasel-family relatives.

Because the fisher is fairly scarce and nocturnal, and prefers wild mature forests, you will be very lucky to sight one in its natural habitat, but it is active year round and its tracks are easy enough to recognize. Typical of the weasel clan, all five toes and claws usually leave imprints, as do the rather narrow pads. Fisher tracks generally lead to or away from trees and avoid water. Walking stride is 10 to 15 inches, with clusters of running tracks 3 to 4 feet apart and 4 to 6 feet between leaping pairs of overlapping prints in the common weasel mode.

Fisher
life size in mud

55

PORCUPINE
Porky, quill pig

Erethizon dorsatum

Order: Rodentia (gnawing mammals). **Family:** Erethizontidae (porcupines). **Range and habitat:** widespread throughout all Rocky Mountain states; usually in forested areas, also in brushy fringes, fields, meadows, and semidesert areas; a very adaptable animal. **Size and weight:** 30 inches; 25 pounds. **Diet:** vegetarian, including bark, leaves, fruits, berries, nuts, flowers. **Sounds:** normally quiet; capable of a great variety of grunts, whines, and harmonicalike noises and rapid teeth clicking.

The porcupine is one of the few animals whose tracks you can follow with reasonable expectation of catching up with their maker. Often out during daylight hours, it moves quite slowly if not alarmed, stops frequently to nibble at vegetation, and does not see well, so if you're quiet, you can usually observe this peaceable animal at your and its leisure. An alarmed porcupine climbs a tree to escape danger, only using its quills as a last-ditch defense against an outright attack; and the porcupine cannot fling its quills, so there's no danger to any creature with enough sense to stay out of direct contact, a requisite that regrettably excludes many domestic dogs.

Often the porcupine's distinctive shuffling gait and dragging whisk-broom tail may be the only clear track signs it leaves behind, especially in deep snow. In winter, porcupine trails often lead to or away from a large coniferous tree, where the animal both sleeps and dines on bark and needles; alternatively, it may hole up in a den beneath a stump or in another ground-level shelter. Occasionally a piece of snow or mud that has stuck to a porcupine's foot will dislodge intact, revealing the unique pebbled texture of its soles. Imprints from the long claws are also often visible.

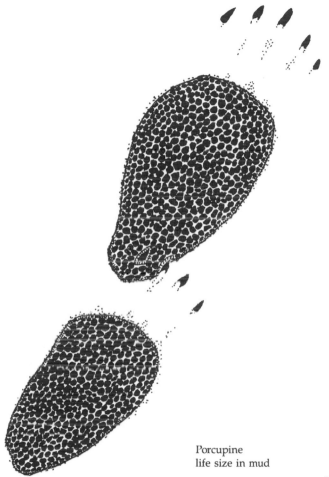

Porcupine
life size in mud

57

RACCOON
Coon

Procyon lotor

Order: Carnivora (flesh-eating mammals). **Family:** Procyonidae (raccoons, ringtails, and coatis). **Range and habitat:** portions of all Rocky Mountain states; in forest fringe and rocky areas near streams, ponds, and lakes. **Size and weight:** 36 inches; 25 pounds. **Diet:** omnivorous, including fish, amphibians, shellfish, insects, birds, eggs, mice, carrion, berries, nuts, and vegetation. **Sounds:** a variety of shrill cries, whistles, churrs, growls, and screeches.

From childhood most of us know the raccoon by its mask of black fur and its black tail stripes on an otherwise grayish brown body. It's familiar as a character in kids' books and frontier lore, frequently seen as a road kill, and is both curious and bold enough to be a fairly common visitor to campgrounds and even residential homes nearly everywhere within its range. Chiefly nocturnal, raccoons are more commonly sighted in suburban neighborhoods raiding garbage cans and terrorizing family hounds than in wildlands. Interesting and intelligent animals with manual dexterity of great renown, raccoons are also reputed to make lively and intriguing pets, provided they are closely supervised.

Raccoons like to wash or tear food items apart in water, which apparently improves their manual sensitivity. Much of their food comes from aquatic prospecting, so you will often find their tracks near water. When a raccoon walks, its left rear foot is placed next to the right front foot, and so forth, forming paired track clusters. On firm mud or dirt, you will likely find tracks like those on the right, with distinct print details. On softer surfaces, they will look more like those on the left. Running-track clusters tend to be bunched irregularly. The walking stride of a raccoon is about 7 inches; leaps average 20 inches.

The ringtail could be mistaken for a raccoon at a quick glimpse. The ringtail's body is more foxlike, its face has white eye rings rather than a black mask, and its tail has black *and white* stripes. It overlaps the raccoon's range, living in Utah, Colorado, New Mexico, and Arizona. You may find the ringtail's tracks near water, as with the raccoon's but the tracks are about the size and shape of a mink.

Raccoon
life size in mud

RIVER OTTER
Land otter

Lutra canadensis

Order: Carnivora (flesh-eating mammals). **Family:** Mustelidae (the weasel family). **Range and habitat:** widespread throughout all Rocky Mountain states; in and near lakes and streams. **Size and weight:** 48 inches; 25 pounds. **Diet:** fish, amphibians, shellfish and other aquatic invertebrates, snakes, turtles, birds, eggs. **Sounds:** chirps, chatters, chuckles, grunts, and growls.

The river otter is a dark brown weasel about as large as a medium-sized dog, with a thick, hairless tail adapted for swimming, much like that of the muskrat; in fact, the river otter closely resembles the muskrat in appearance and habitat, but is much larger, strictly carnivorous, and quite a bit more animated. Both in and out of water, alone or in the company of others, the river otter seems to be a graceful and exuberant playful animal. Active during the daylight hours, the otter is wary of humans. Still, you might occasionally sight one in the wild; more commonly you may find, in summer, the flattened grass where otters have rolled, leaving their musky odor behind, or in winter, marks on snow or ice where they've playfully slid on their bellies.

River otter tracks are relatively easy to find and identify within the otter's range. The webs of the rear feet often leave distinct marks on soft surfaces, and claw marks usually are present. Individual tracks measure up to 3.5 inches across and due to their size cannot be confused with those of any other animal with similar aquatic habitat. River otters do venture into woodlands as well, however, where small otter tracks could be mistaken for those of a large fisher, but fisher tracks will lead to or from coniferous trees before long, in somewhat more linear patterns, while otter tracks meander, forming a trail roughly 8 to 10 inches wide and generally leading to or from water systems. Also, the river otter normally leaves groups of four tracks 13 to 30 inches apart, when it's not sliding on its belly.

River Otter
life size in mud

61

LYNX
Felis lynx

Order: Carnivora (flesh-eating mammals). **Family:** Felidae (cats). **Range and habitat:** portions of Idaho, Montana, Wyoming, Colorado, and Utah, absent from New Mexico and Arizona; in forested woodlands and swamp fringes, wherever the snowshoe hare is found. **Size and weight:** 36 inches; 30 pounds. **Diet:** primarily snowshoe hares; occasionally other small mammals and birds. **Sounds:** quite vocal, including hisses, spitting noises, growls, caterwauls, and other generic cat family noises.

Closely related to the bobcat in both size and characteristics, the lynx has adapted to its generally more northerly range with longer legs, longer and denser fur, and larger, thickly furred paws that provide buoyancy in deep snow and make them excellent swimmers; conspicuous black ear tufts also distinguish it from the bobcat, whose range it does overlap. The lynx relies on snowshoe hares as its dietary mainstay, and its range precisely overlaps the wilder, more remote portions of the hare's range. When the cyclical hare population is at a peak, lynxes have larger litters, but when the hares are scarce, the cats bear fewer offspring. The lynx hunts on the ground, but will go into trees to catch prey or to wait for ground animals to pass beneath.

The wary lynx is most active at night; by day, it tends to rest somewhere, venturing out only to kill unlucky prey that happens by, so you will seldom see it in the wild, but its tracks are unique, clearly larger than those of the bobcat. The range of the lynx also overlaps that of the mountain lion. Their feet are roughly the same size, but lynx trails are only about 7 or 8 inches wide, and its walking stride is around 12 inches. The lynx is also much lighter than the mountain lion, causing shallower tracks on yielding surfaces.

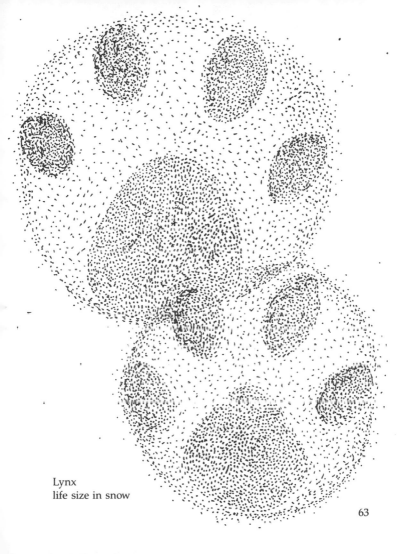

Lynx
life size in snow

PRONGHORN
Antelope

Antilocapra americana

Order: Artiodactyla (even-toed hoofed mammals). **Family:** Antilocapridae (pronghorns). **Range and habitat:** portions of all Rocky Mountain states; on open prairies and sagebrush plains; especially common in Yellowstone and Wind Cave national parks and in Petrified Forest National Park. **Height and weight:** 36 inches at shoulder; 120 pounds. **Diet:** vegetation, including weeds, shrubs, grasses, and herbs; fond of sagebrush. **Sounds:** usually silent, but capable of a loud whistling sound when startled.

The pronghorn is the most easily observed of the Rocky Mountain hoofed mammals. This sociable animal lives in flat open country, and its tan hide marked with striking white rump patches, a white underside, and facial spots is easy to spot. The fastest animals in North America, pronghorns race around the prairies en masse at speeds of 45 miles per hour or so.

Because the pronghorn is easily sighted from a distance, you normally won't have to rely on tracks for field identification, but the tracks should be easy to recognize because, unlike the mule and the white-tailed deer, which share much of its range, the pronghorn has no dewclaws. It is more gregarious than deer, and its running characteristics are unique: a large group of pronghorn may run for a mile or more in a straight line, whereas deer tend to run only when startled, and then they don't run very far. The pronghorn's great speed produces an average separation of 14 feet between track clusters; running white-tailed deer average 6 feet, and mule deer average about 10 feet.

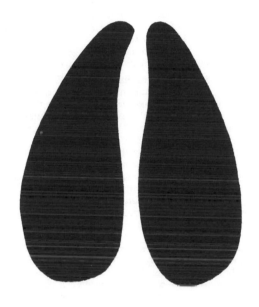

Pronghorn
life size in mud

WHITE-TAILED DEER
Whitetail, Virginia deer

Odocoileus virginianus

Order: Artiodactyla (even-toed hoofed mammals). **Family:** Cervidae (deer). **Range and habitat:** Idaho and Montana southward through eastern Colorado to northern New Mexico; in deciduous and mixed woodlands and nearby river bottomlands, creeksides, open brushy areas, and swamp fringes. **Height and weight:** 42 inches at shoulder; 250 pounds. **Diet:** browse from shrubs and lower tree limbs; less frequently fungi, nuts, grains, grasses, and herbs. **Sounds:** low bleats, guttural grunts, snorts, and whistles of alarm.

The white-tailed deer is recognizable in the wild by the all-white underside of its tail, which the animal raises prominently when it runs. It usually has a home range of only a square mile or so, although some migrate to swamps in cold weather. White-tailed deer usually gather in groups of no more than 3 animals, except in the dead of winter when the group may swell to 25. They spend their days browsing and quietly chewing their cud and when startled run only short distances to the nearest cover.

The white-tailed deer's range overlaps that of many other deer species, but its tracks are easy enough to identify. Individual tracks are relatively long and slender, averaging about 3 inches in length; the dewclaws will leave prints in snow or soft earth. Taken alone, a single track could be confused with one left by a mule deer, but when running, the white-tailed deer tends to trot rather than bound, often leaving tracks in a more or less straight line, with up to 6 feet between track groups. Its walking gait is less than 20 inches, with tracks frequently doubled up, as the rear feet cover prints left by the front. Also, the white-tailed deer generally lives in open forests and upland meadows, whereas the mule deer prefers either more mountainous terrain or open prairies and desert plains.

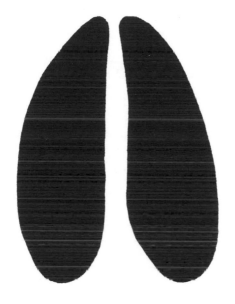

White-tailed Deer
life size in mud

MULE DEER   *Odocoileus hemionus*

Order: Artiodactyla (even-toed hoofed mammals). **Family:** Cervidae (deer). **Range and habitat:** widespread throughout all Rocky Mountain states; coniferous forests and adjoining areas at all elevations, regularly moving into grasslands, chaparral, and desert fringes that have browse plants available. **Height and weight:** 42 inches at shoulder; 350 pounds. **Diet:** herbivorous, including leaves, grasses, grains, nuts, and berries. **Sounds:** generally silent, but produces a blowing, snorting whistle when alarmed; makes occasional grunts and other vocal noises.

Often ranging into more open or mountainous country than that chosen by the white-tailed deer, the mule deer of the Rockies is a heavier and stockier deer easily recognized by its large ears and black-tipped tail, which it keeps down when running, as opposed to the upraised, white flag-tail of the white-tailed deer. Active during the day and at dusk, the mule deer can be observed fairly often in the wild. Skittish, at the first sign of alarm it flees with a unique feet-together bounding gait, all four hooves landing and taking off at the same time. The mule deer is also a strong swimmer.

Mule deer tracks show small, slender hooves usually spread slightly at the heels and, often, dewclaw impressions. The doubled-over walking tracks are usually less than 2 feet apart; at speeds beyond a walk, the mule deer does not trot like the white-tailed deer, but bounds, leaving very distinctive clusters of parallel tracks 10 feet or more apart.

Mule Deer
life size in mud

MOUNTAIN GOAT   *Oreamnos americanus*

Order: Artiodactyla (even-toed hoofed mammals). **Family:** Bovidae (cattle, sheep, and goats). **Range and habitat:** northern Idaho and northwest Montana; mountainous, steep, high-altitude pastures near or between cliff sections, usually just below snowline. **Height and weight:** 42 inches at shoulder; 300 pounds. **Diet:** grasses, leaves, lichens, and other alpine vegetation. **Sounds:** generally silent.

The mountain goat, a stocky, heavily muscled animal with a white fur coat and short black horns, has hooves superbly adapted for the mountainous terrain in which it lives. The combination of a hard outer edge and a flexible inner pad affords the animal the equivalent of rock-climbing boots, and the only thing that can catch a healthy mountain goat in its extremely steep habitat is another goat. But even mountain goats hit loose holds now and then, and the resulting falls are often fatal. Consequently, they prefer to graze high alpine pastures, with a sentry or two posted. The herd, which may number 12 or more animals scattered widely, returns to the rocks only when necessary to escape wolves, mountain lions, biting flies, or wildlife photographers, none of which bother them to any great extent.

Mountain goat tracks are fairly common near high alpine ponds and in patches of dirt around the rocky areas it inhabits. Winter snows often force the mountain goat down into deer country, but its tracks are generally distinctive and identifiable: the hooves are usually longer than those of deer and more pointed and splayed than those of the bighorn sheep; dewclaw imprints are absent. The mountain goat tends to climb rocks carefully, generally keeping its hooves sharp, whereas in my experience the bighorn sheep scuffs its hooves around on scree slopes, making the hooves more blocky, blunt, and broken.

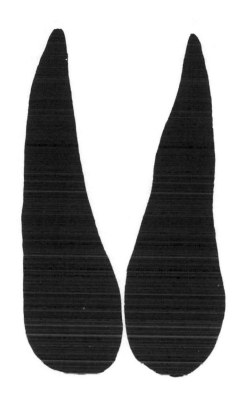

Mountain Goat
life size in mud

BIGHORN SHEEP   *Ovis canadensis*
Rocky Mountain bighorn, mountain sheep

Order: Artiodactyla (even-toed hoofed mammals). **Family:** Bovidae (cattle, sheep, and goats). **Range and habitat:** portions of all Rocky Mountain states, especially common in Yellowstone and Glacier national parks; in mountainous, sparsely populated terrain and high hilly desert, avoiding forested areas. **Height and weight:** 45 inches at shoulder; 275 pounds. **Diet:** variety of high-altitude browse, grasses, herbs, lichens. **Sounds:** most recognizable and voluminous are the sounds of head and horn butting made by competing rams during late fall; coughs, grunts, bleating.

This big sheep, with its distinctive white rump and heavy coiled horns, lives in remote areas of the Rockies, where its hooves with their hard outer edge and spongy center give it excellent agility on rocky surfaces. It tends, however, to prefer high mountain meadows and scree slopes. In the summer, you commonly see groups of about ten ewes and lambs grazing or lying around chewing their cuds. In winter, rams join the herd, which may grow in size to 100 animals or more. The most distinctive behavior of the bighorn sheep is the frenzied, high-speed head butting engaged in by competing rams before the autumn mating season; noise from the impact carries a great distance in the open mountain country. Thanks to a certain American truck manufacturer's television ads, people have had the opportunity to witness this head-butting ram ritual without having to venture into remote mountainous wildlands, thus saving wear and tear on fragile ecosystems and human knee joints.

Because of the habitat where they are commonly found, bighorn sheep tracks are rarely confused with those of other deer species. The hooves average 3.5 inches in length, longer than those of other deer but not as big as those of the elk. Rather blunt and square, the hooves may show signs of wear and tear from the scree slopes; dewclaw prints are never left.

Bighorn Sheep
life size in mud

ELK
Wapiti

Cervus elaphus

Order: Artiodactyla (even-toed hoofed mammals). **Family:** Cervidae (deer). **Range and habitat:** portions of all Rocky Mountain states, but rare in northern Arizona and New Mexico; in mountains, foothills, plains, valley meadows, and fringes of semiopen forests; at higher altitudes in summer than winter. **Height and weight:** 60 inches at shoulder; 900 pounds. **Diet:** leaves, grasses, bark, grains, and other vegetation. **Sounds:** variety of squeals, grunts, and barking exhalations; distinctive bugle call during autumn mating.

Second in size only to the moose among Rocky Mountain deer species, the elk is a herd animal whose numbers have been drastically reduced by hunters over the last century. Today Rocky Mountain states support most of the remaining herds of elk on the continent. The cow elk does not have the impressive multispiked antlers of the adult male, but all elk can be recognized easily: significantly larger than the white-tailed and mule deer but not as massive as the familiar moose, the elk has a mane noticeably darker than its body, yellowish-white rump patches, and a small white tail.

Within the Rocky Mountain states, elk and moose ranges do overlap, but you should have no problem differentiating elk tracks, which are bigger than those of deer but smaller than those of the moose. Individual elk tracks measure as much as 4.5 inches in length; the dewclaws may not leave imprints when the elk is walking, but on softer surfaces or when running, the elk's sheer weight drives its legs down, and the dewclaw prints will be apparent. The elk's walking gait measures from 25 to 30 inches; clusters of running tracks may be 4 to 8 feet apart. Shallow ponds and mud wallows are the best places to find elk tracks during the months when snow is absent.

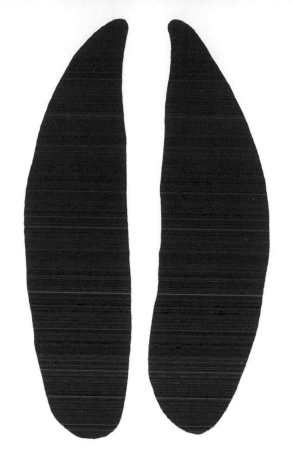

Elk
life size in mud

BISON   *Bison bison*
Buffalo

Order: Artiodactyla (even-toed hoofed mammals). **Family:** Bovidae (cattle, sheep, and goats). **Range and habitat:** isolated herds throughout all Rocky Mountain states, especially in Yellowstone, Platt, and Wind Cave national parks, House Rock Valley in Colorado, and National Bison Range in Montana; on open plains, grasslands, and occasionally in woodlands and woodland fringes in northern areas. **Height and weight:** 72 inches at shoulder; 2000 pounds. **Diet:** grazes mostly on grass; occasionally browses for buds, bark, twigs, shoots, and other vegetation. **Sounds:** a range of bovine noises.

Their dark brown, shaggy mane and beard, massive humped shoulders, and sharp, stout, upturned horns make the great plains bison unmistakable. In 1880 more than 40 million bison grazed peacefully and stolidly in America, seldom taking notice of humans. Today there are 100,000 bison in the United States, largely captive and controlled in ten major public herds and many smaller private ones.

Bison are quite gregarious animals, with herd sizes numbering in the thousands. It's a mistake to read meekness into the bison's seemingly mild-mannered indifference, however, because bison are huge and quick, quick enough to outrun a horse over a quarter-mile course. It's a good idea to treat a bison with the same respect and common sense you would any large, domestic bull. Statistics reveal, for example, that in Yellowstone a hiker is more likely to be injured by a bison than to even sight a grizzly.

Chances are that you will know you are in bison territory and see the animals long before you find their tracks. Nevertheless, the tracks are a unique shape and size, measuring roughly 5 inches in each direction, with about 25 to 30 inches between walking track clusters. Bison also like to roll around, forming prominent dust wallows on the plains.

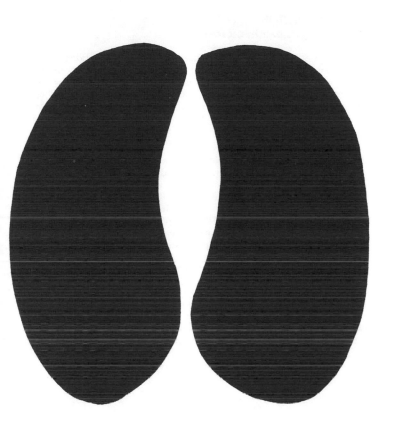

Bison
¾ life size in mud

MOUNTAIN LION   *Felis concolor*
Puma, cougar, panther, catamount

Order: Carnivora (flesh-eating mammals). **Family:** Felidae (cats).
Range and habitat: throughout all Rocky Mountain states, mostly
along and west of the Continental Divide; in rugged wilderness
mountains, forests, and swamp fringes. **Size and weight:** 84 inches;
200 pounds. **Diet:** primarily deer, small mammals, and birds; occasionally domestic animals. **Sounds:** generally quiet, but capable of a
variety of voluminous feline screams, hisses, and growls.

Hunted to the verge of extinction, our large, tawny, native American cat with its long, waving tail is now so scarce and secretive and is
confined to such remote terrain that you'd be very lucky to sight one
in the wild. But you at least have a chance to find the tracks of this big
cat, which hunts mostly on the ground. It occasionally climbs trees,
particularly to evade dogs but also to drop onto unwary prey (the
mountain lion is an important natural control of the deer population).

Mountain lion tracks are similar in size to those of the lynx, but
may be distinguished by the angular shape of the pads and the absence of excessive fur around the toes; on soft surfaces the mountain
lion sinks deeper, too. Spacing of tracks will also be what you'd expect of the large cat: trail width of 12 inches or more, walking tracks
over 20 inches apart, 3 feet separating pairs of loping tracks, and
bounding leaps of 12 feet or more. Another sure sign is the tail drag
marks that may be found, especially in snow. Of course, like most
cats, the mountain lion has retractile claws, which never leave marks.

Mountain Lion
life size in mud

MOUNTAIN COTTONTAIL
Nuttall's cottontail

Sylvilagus nuttalli

Order: Lagomorpha (rabbitlike mammals). **Family:** Leporidae (hares and rabbits). **Range and habitat:** portions of all Rocky Mountain states; in mountainous sagebrush, thickets, rocky areas, and forests, often extending into outskirts of urban areas. **Size and weight:** 13 inches; 3 pounds. **Diet:** green vegetation, bark, twigs, sagebrush, and juniper berries. **Sounds:** usually silent; loud squeal when extremely distressed.

Cottontails are the pudgy, adorable rabbits with cottonball tails, known to us all from childhood tales of Peter Rabbit. Active day and night, year round, they're generally plentiful due in part to the fact that each adult female produces three or four litters of four to seven young rabbits every year. Of course, a variety of predators helps control their numbers, and few live more than a year in the wild.

Cottontail tracks are easily recognized because the basic pattern doesn't vary much, regardless of the rabbit's speed. It's important to note that, as with all rabbit-family tracks, sometimes the front feet land together, side by side, but just as often the second fore foot lands in line ahead of the first. The mountain cottontail leaves track clusters that span 6 and 9 inches normally, with up to 3 feet between running clusters.

Of the three species of cottontail rabbits found in the Rocky Mountain states, the mountain cottontail is the most widespread and abundant. The eastern cottontail lives east of the Continental Divide and in southern New Mexico and Arizona, a range that excludes the mountain cottontail. The desert cottontail inhabits lowland plains, valleys, and foothills. The pygmy rabbit lives in clumps of sagebrush in southern Idaho and western Utah.

You will have no problem telling cottontail tracks from those of jackrabbits, whose track clusters span as much as 2 feet, with up to 20 feet separating clusters; and because jackrabbits tend to run up on the toes of their hind feet, they often leave *smaller* hind foot imprints than cottontails do. The comparably great size of the snowshoe hare's feet makes its tracks easy to distinguish.

Mountain Cottontail
life size in snow

BLACK-TAILED JACKRABBIT
Jackass rabbit

Lepus californicus

Order: Lagomorpha (rabbitlike mammals). **Family:** Leporidae (hares and rabbits). **Range and habitat:** all states except Montana, northern Idaho, and Wyoming; in open prairies and sparsely vegetated sage and cactus country. **Size and weight:** 20 inches; 6 pounds. **Diet:** mostly grasses and other green vegetation, often along highway edges; also shrubs, buds, bark, twigs, and cultivated crops. **Sounds:** normally silent.

The black-tailed jackrabbit, the most widespread and numerous jackrabbit of the western plains, is easily recognized by its year-round light gray fur, white underside, and distinctive black fur patch on top of its tail. It is most active from dusk to dawn and spends most of its days lying in depressions it scoops out at the base of a bush, by a rock, or at any other spot that gives it a bit of protection. These jackrabbits are sociable and are often seen feeding in small groups.

The white-tailed jackrabbit is found on the northern plains and western hills of Montana and Wyoming and overlaps the range of the black-tailed jackrabbit in southern Idaho, Utah, and Colorado. The tracks of both are indistinguishable where their ranges overlap. Front prints, about 3 inches long, are usually compact but often splayed, as shown; are usually the same size regardless of speed, and fall behind the rear, a pattern typical of all rabbits. Hind prints vary greatly in size. Walking slowly and flat-footed, jackrabbits leave narrow rear prints about 6 inches long, but as speed increases, heels lift until, at top speed of 35 to 40 miles per hour, only the toes leave prints, about 3.5 inches long, sometimes resembling coyote tracks.

Jackrabbit tracks cannot be confused with those of the snowshoe hare, which overlaps the ranges of both jackrabbits, because it prefers forested rather than open terrain and because its toes are bigger and usually spread apart leaving larger imprints.

The most distinguishing track characteristic of jackrabbits is that, at speed, they leap from 7 to 12 feet or more. Coyotes and snowshoe hares rarely leap more than 6 feet, and cottontails bound no more than 3 feet.

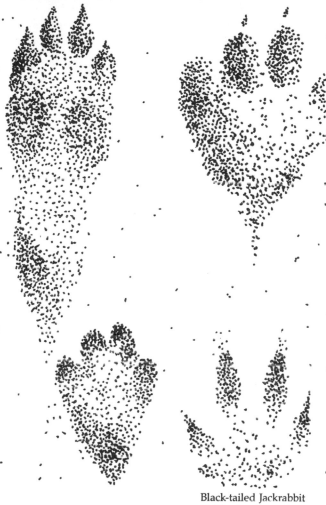

Black-tailed Jackrabbit
½ life size in sand

MOOSE

Alces alces

Order: Artiodactyla (even-toed hoofed mammals). **Family:** Cervidae (deer). **Range:** Montana, Idaho, Wyoming, northern Utah, and Colorado; in meadows, lake and swamp fringes, and brushy thickets; less common in forested areas. **Height and weight:** 72 inches at shoulder; 1100 pounds. **Diet:** aquatic plants, leafy succulents, twigs, bark, terminal shoots, and other vegetation. **Sounds:** generally silent, but may make a variety of whines, bellows, grunts, and other guttural noises.

Like all ruminant animals, the moose spends most of its waking hours slowly moving about and chewing. Its normal response to perceived threat is to gallop wildly a few hundred feet on legs wonderfully adapted for running through high, thick brush, then to stop and resume its cud-chewing. Be that as it may, the bull moose does put on quite a display in the autumn, jousting with massive antlers; but beware, it can be quite unpredictably aggressive toward humans at that time of year, as can a cow with a young calf in spring.

Differentiating the tracks of the smaller speices of the deer family can be problematic at times, but not so with adult moose tracks, which are strikingly large, from 5 to 7 inches long and up to 4 feet apart when the animal is merely walking. Juvenile moose tracks, however, can be confused with elk or mule deer tracks, so search the vicinity for the larger tracks of an accompanying adult. Habitat will be a clue, also, because no other deer species shares the moose's great affinity for water.

Finally, the moose is not a herd animal. A moose gathering is generally no larger than a bull, cow, and two calves, whereas mule deer and elk often congregate in larger numbers. Then again, a few moose can make a lot of tracks hanging around a small pond for an extended period of time, which they do. In that case, though, the largeness of the adult tracks will provide positive identification.

Moose
½ life size in mud

GRAY WOLF
Timber wolf

Canis lupus

Order: Carnivora (flesh-eating mammals). **Family:** Canidae (dogs).
Range and habitat: uncommon in remote northern portions of Idaho
and Montana, possibly as far south as southeast Utah and southwest
Colorado; in forested and open areas, to far above timberline. **Size
and weight:** 72 inches; 110 pounds. **Diet:** primarily deer as well as
smaller mammals down to mice; occasionally berries, birds, eggs,
and insects. **Sounds:** variety of canine noises, including barks,
snarls, and growls; occasionally various howls, solo or in chorus,
often of lengthy duration.

You can consider yourself fortunate indeed if you sight a gray wolf
in the wild these days, for they have been systematically extermi-
nated from nearly all the contiguous 48 states.

The gray wolf, an intelligent, gregarious animal that mates for life
and has quite complicated social organizations, would seem to
deserve protection from eradication. Gray wolves pose no threat to
humans.

You may not see the wary wolf, but its tracks are out there to be
found and identified in its remote mountain habitats. Wolf tracks
show the four toes and nails typical of the canine family, with the
front foot slightly larger than the rear. Angularity of pads, inner toes
slightly larger than outer, and overall dimensions distinguish wolf
tracks; no other canine is likely to leave tracks 5 inches or more in
length in remote wilderness areas, and no other canine covers
ground like the gray wolf, with its walking stride of nearly 30 inches
and leaps of 9 feet or more.

Gray Wolf
½ life size in mud

SNOWSHOE HARE
Varying hare

Lepus americanus

Order: Lagomorpha (rabbitlike mammals). **Family:** Leporidae (hares and rabbits). **Range and habitat:** widespread from Canadian border to northern New Mexico, rare in northern Arizona; in mountainous forests, brush thickets, and swamp fringes. **Size and weight:** 18 inches; 4 pounds. **Diet:** succulent vegetation in summer, twigs, bark, and buds in winter; occasionally eats frozen meat. **Sounds:** generally silent; may thump feet, scream, grunt, or growl occasionally.

This medium-sized member of the rabbit family is active day and night year round and is quite common over a large territory within its preferred habitat. The animal has two color phases: medium brown in summer months, molting in winter to white—sometimes slightly mottled with brown—with black ear tips. Aptly named, its unique heavily furred hind feet have separable toes, allowing them to function like snowshoes when the hare is traveling on soft surfaces, especially deep snow.

Although its range partially overlaps that of both the cottontail and the jackrabbit, track recognition is easy because of the natural snowshoe formed by its toes. A snowshoe hare's toes always spread out, leaving distinctively separate imprints. Track measurements lie between the cottontail's and jackrabbit's: the length of each track cluster of four prints averages 11 inches; hopping distance is about 14 inches, and leaps are more than 5 feet.

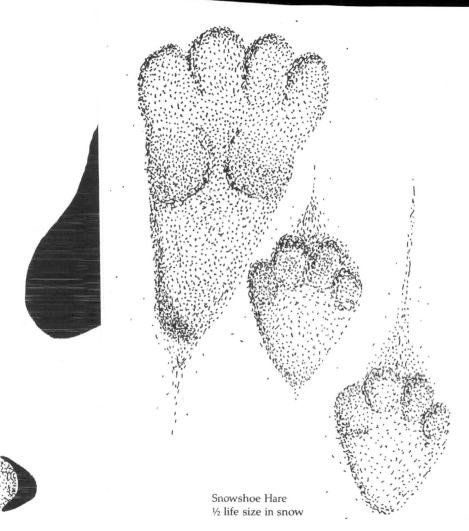

Snowshoe Hare
½ life size in snow

89

BLACK BEAR

Order: Carniv
Range and hab
ily in medium-t
fringes. **Size and**
cluding smaller
and succulent pl
woof, whimper,
mediately recogn

The black bear
You may have see
parks. In the wild,
a general rule and
however, it can be
is very strong, agi
25 miles per hour
able. The black be
has been known to

Be alert for bear
trees with claw m
tracks are usually e
and size but slightl
toes do. If a bear
smooth slide mark
tracks. Both adult l
about 7 inches, but
the grizzly bear. Kn
two species, conver
pertise, and field
species you are likel
fication efforts. If th
similar but smaller t
black bear and its of
certainly made by an

About the author:

Chris Stall first became interested in wild country and wild animals during several years with a very active Boy Scout troop in rural New York State. In the two decades since then he has travelled and lived around most of North America, studying, photographing, sketching and writing about wild animals in their natural habitats. His photos and articles have appeared in a number of outdoor and nature magazines. Stall currently lives in Cincinnati, his launching point for a 1365-mile solo kayak journey down the Mississippi River to New Orleans in 1988.

Look for these other "natural items" from The Mountaineers:

MAC'S FIELD GUIDES
This series of plastic laminated cards can be easily fit in a pack, taped to a kayak deck, dropped in the sand, marked with crayons or grease pencil and still keep on giving great information. Developed by a teacher of marine science, these field guides have color drawings to readily identify a wide array of wildlife, complete with both common and scientific names, and information on size and habitat. Each card: $4.95

Subjects include freshwater and coastal fish, coastal invertebrates, coastal and park/backyard birds, cactus and wildflowers, land and marine mammals, reptiles, and birds of prey. The areas represented by individual cards include the Northeast, the Northwest, Rocky Mountains, the Southwest, and California.

For a complete listing of these cards in a catalog of more than 200 outdoor books, write to:

THE MOUNTAINEERS
1011 S.W. Klickitat Way
Seattle, WA   98134